uninhibited
beat poetry

elliot m rubin

Library of Congress
Copyright November 2024
ISBN # 978-8-9922464-0-7
EPUB # 979-8-9990376-1-9

Library of Congress Control Number: 2024926887

Published 2025

Published by
elliot m rubin

Dedication

To my grandchildren
Shane, Isabelle, Jonathan, Carter,
Alexandra, Melanie, Mollie, and Madison

In memory of my father

Herman S. Rubin
who wrote poetry, prayers and letters all his life

Special thanks to

Charlene Brown
for her help in editing this book

Preface

I believe poetry is to be read and understood by all, and it needs to be written, for the most part, in plain language for everyone's enjoyment.

Too often, poets write in-depth, penetrating poems where you need to be well-read and/or versed in literary minutia to appreciate the poetry, not this book or any of my writings. I try to write so everyone can enjoy a few moments of intellectual satisfaction without consulting a dictionary or encyclopedia all the time.

Disclaimer

This book of poetry is not intended to be read by prudes, political book-banning conservatives, and/or sexually inhibited and repressed small-minded dolts.

No human models were caught, used, or harmed in making the cover; it is AI-generated, at random.

What is Progressive Beat Poetry

Progressive beat poetry is a type of poetry that goes against the usual rules and traditions. It talks about social, political, and cultural issues to make people more aware and push for change. Here are some key points about progressive poetry:

- **Questioning the Norms**: Progressive beat poets often challenge and question the main social, political, and cultural ideas. They dive into complex topics like race, gender, and power.
- **Voices and Inclusion**: This poetry style aims to give a voice to those who are often ignored. It highlights stories and experiences that don't usually get attention.
- **Thinking and Talking**: Progressive beat poetry makes readers think about bigger societal issues and encourages meaningful conversations. It aims to start discussions and inspire actions towards social justice.
- **Breaking the Mold**: Progressive poets often play with form and structure, moving away from traditional styles to better express their messages.

Progressive beat poetry seeks to break free from traditional poetic conventions and push the boundaries of language, space-as-art, and expression.

Table of Contents

atomic bomb 1955

in elementary school
we had air raid drills
i grew up
terrified of the bomb
the fucking russians had one, too
they said they have as many as us
and can blow up the world
many times over
they were bloodthirsty, red commies,
who didn't care about life or freedom
russkies had no god   or fear —
we'd bend onto our knees
to scrunch under
a fifty-year-old wooden desk
with carvings on top
of previous lovelorn students —
had to tuck down
avoid old gum stuck underneath
put hands over heads;
my desk, with a steel frame
bolted to the floor
was supposed to save me
though the building
would be blown to ash,
but that fucking desk,
and stern, never smiling, mrs white
standing, arms crossed, in front of the class
would still be there in one piece —
they don't make desks like that anymore
or indestructible, indomitable teachers

never marry a tercet

how can you dance
with a three-legged stanza
it's something so odd

which word has the rhyme
there is no alternating thing
like a quatrain with a ring

forget italian, miltonic, or curtal,
shakespearean, and spenserian too
even kirche's modern sonnet a no-go

if the first line's end rhyme
is to marry the second, no crime,
maybe a couplet is your chosen form

but if three is your first choice
polyamory might be your thing
to set you free to poetically swing

waiting for the service writer (a riff on Godot)

i sit in the waiting area
alone
an early saturday morning appointment
cars need service occasionally
waiting for the service writer
a tall, heavy-set man walks in
wears a large, wide-brimmed hat
are you the service writer i ask
    no, i'm on my way to the restroom
    do you know where it is
sorry i'm just waiting for the service writer
    guess I'll have to look around for it he replied
he left the waiting area
i'm alone again

a young woman walks in with a seeing-eye dog
    are you the service writer she asks
no, sorry, i'm waiting for him, too
i begin to wonder to myself
how did she drive here if she can't see
i don't ask her, the dog is big, and
has large tartar-stained teeth
    i'm going to look in the back for him the woman
said
the dog leads her away, out of the waiting area

the tall heavy-set man
with the wide-brimmed hat comes back
his pants are wet
    i didn't find the restroom

i don't think they have one here
he said good luck to me, then he leaves, too

in a few minutes, the dog comes back
alone
he is a big dog
now with milky, glazed eyes, as a blind dog with
cataracts would have
i sit still, not a smile or muscle do i move
minutes later, the blind woman walks in,
she is wearing very thick bottle-like lens glasses
i didn't find the service writer, guess
he isn't in yet, i am going to go home
alone again
i'm still waiting for the service writer

belief

she sees him
in church on sundays
seven feet tall on a cross
bleeding, plaster white skin
hanging on the wall
behind the altar
only inches from the priest
as he leads prayers —
her innermost turmoil not soothed
when she leaves a hardwood pew
doesn't think he hears her desires
in church, or helps celestially

not even mom's front yard madonna assists
even when nonna crosses herself
whispers rosary bead by bead —
only the tiny, hand-held, palm-sized
plastic baby jesus with arms extended
hears her desperate pleas for help —

yet the small toy
from an old christmas manger
a gift from heaven
tells her to live life fully —
tomorrow, she believes,
will be better because baby jesus,
always in her pocket
can save her from self-harm

soul singer

young
not married
three babies in the crib
bill collectors at the door
baby daddy is no more
social worker visits often
welfare checks buy some food
government wants her to work
what to do
what to do
she sings songs at a laundromat
while doing her weekly wash and dry
music's in her soul
without it, she would die
life's not easy to make ends meet
a hopeless victim
of a man's deceit

daily walks

ideally,
i'd walk through dark
overgrown woods
on a well-worn dirt path
during a sudden warm spell
instead of kept indoors in winter
with snow piled high on sidewalks
impossible to go to work

my kitchen is oven-warm
with baked cakes rising
as my lover mixes and stirs
fully undressed
when she asks me
to join her in there
knowing full well
my yeast can rise
and licks the spare icing
before she washes up

can't go home again

it's been over sixty years since we last dated
we were an item back then
high school sweethearts
we danced to the beat of a different drummer
i played guitar and bass in garage bands
she was my groupie
pink hair everywhere
yes, even there, as we
walked greenwich village streets
in the city, hung out in late-night hot spots
near new york university on east 8th street
in apartment-building basements
where music played all night   and
we weed-smoked, bodies reeked, air stunk,
and free love a life choice
on an old, lice-ridden floor mattress

thought i saw her last week by sheer chance
on a train to the city —
grey-haired, hunched over,
wore old, black, high-top sneakers, white socks,
with a long madras skirt;
saw her smile, some front teeth missing,
and a cane kept her upright —
i didn't say hello, because sometimes

memories are too valuable to lose

modernism

he needs a model
for a painting he wants to do
in a modern media method
of lines, circles, color slashes

she answers an ad

when she agrees to his terms
she undresses
her fully feminine form features
a fluffy, full tummy and
boasts bulbous breasts
declaring to all her self-confidence

exposed to a discerning eye
tubes of acrylic squeeze out
on a palette secured in his hand —
the brush's bristles twirl in small strokes
a new mix of hues splash on canvas
one after the other, a form appears,
when his creative tenseness rises
and needs a release
she beckons him to her;
his picture will wait
while he sojourns with her
to a land of ecstasy

loving daughter
published in Heron Clan XII literary journal

she wanted her space
to be left alone
too much nagging from mom
who never believed her complaints
desperate for solitude
her diary was her friend
always there
no secrets withheld
even the touching
from boyfriends, step-father
and a high school female nurse,
she hid in her book bag
only a zipper away

through college and marriage
they were replaced
when blank pages disappeared
until the day mom died

she threw all the years of diaries
in the grave with the coffin
burying her trauma
because
she finally sunk into
her quiet space

shopping

i see him in the dairy aisle,
seems lost, like he was never in one
couldn't decide on milk,
fat-free, one or two percent, or whole,
while his wife is home,
wherever that is today,
looking at expensive designer clothes
her stylist, who lives in subsidized housing,
brought for her to try on
while she's in her fifth avenue penthouse

i notice he then walks away
wanders in the fruit section
fondles melons
stormy watches from a distance
offers to spank him again,
but i see he ignores her,
then stops a sixteen-year-old latina girl
with flowing black hair, big breasts, brown eyes
asks
if she'd like to visit a caribbean island
his good friend jeffrey owns
she can *party* in the sun
with both of them,
when a young boy walks past
eating a cheeseburger from mickey d's
the scent tickles his nose,
he leaves to buy a dozen
with a government credit card,
not his own money, of course,

adds fries and five large diet cokes,
then leaves, bypassing homeless old men
who sleep on sidewalks
tells them
i'm going to save the nation money
by cutting social services benefits,
although it won't help you now,
but in the future,
if you ever get their act together

suddenly, he grasps at his chest,
falls to the ground
medics rush over;
they try resuscitation

    nothing happens

then realize
it can't be a heart attack
          he doesn't have one

book signing

not many things in life are free
air if you can breathe it,
water if you can drink it,
that's about it

i work for things
nothing is free
she stops by my book signing
loves my poems
loves my words
wants to love me, too

the bookstore restroom
stall is small
two is too crowded

i found out
if two people get close
        intimately close
it's still a tight space
            but who cares

florida storm

waters rise
hurricane season's here
a category 5 storm on the way
wood and steel shutters closed
people told to leave
twenty-foot surf expected
waters rise higher

police will not come to save you
an old couple in their old home
on the street where they lived fifty years
with no place to go
with no life's savings
who live day to day on social security
waters rise even more

married sixty-three years
water seeps under the door
they lay in bed together
water is now higher and higher
they hold each other's hand
then swallow a fist full of pills
close their eyes after a kiss
water reaches up to the bed

they fall soundly asleep
together forever

memoir of youth

1 - crossing the jordan 1964

back then, i lived in another world growing up
in sheltered middle-class jewish brooklyn, where a date
was a movie or burger deluxe, either in *wolfies* or
cookies restaurants, until college in the city started; then
i began to explore manhattan.

walking in hippie heaven on east eighth street in
greenwich village, i met young abigail with her
floor-length, flowing, rose-colored madras dress, her
long, wavy, waist-length dark hair, unshaved legs and
pits, a firm believer in a free-love religion.

soon, i too converted and discovered the pleasures of
crossing the jordan into the promised land.

2 - abigail

i remember abigail. she lived in a walk-up tenement in manhattan in the hippie, drug-fueled, free love nineteen-sixties.

the community bathroom down the hall, in a 100-year-old plus building, had a musty smell; occasionally, i saw critters dash under the stove for warmth, yet her bed was warmer when she brought me home or when her girlfriend kiesha would visit to help keep the sheets iron-hot. she'd join us in the evenings in a matrimonial manner; later, we all went to dance clubs until dawn, returned high on cocaine, and sometimes with another girl, who made a queen sofa bed rather crowded.

i lost track of her when she moved west to join a commune in taos, new mexico, to study art as an apprentice to a well-known international artist, and to pose as a muse and his lover.

years later, i saw abigail sit naked on a walnut-stained bent-wood chair in a large framed painting in a madison avenue art dealer's window, with her sundress on the floor in front of her unshaved body hair; that picture is worth more than a three-bedroom condo on upper park avenue that sold last year for millions of dollars.

my memories are priceless.

3 - keisha

keisha is biracial, bisexual, and bipolar.

she moved into the apartment as abigail's civil union partner once she went west, and brought her laid back, irish, trans, bisexual boyfriend tomás with her. keisha's highs were fantastic, and those times are treasured. but her lows were so low they had to be institutionalized until the right drug and therapist hit

meanwhile, tomás took over in bed when she was gone. it seemed like nothing changed.

keisha was a jewelry designer with a huge international firm that is well known for light blue boxes filled with expensive jewels. her lover tomás does bike messenger runs all over manhattan; was muscular and takes male hormones daily. but still has female genitalia.

before keisha was institutionalized the first time, i was asked to live with both of them. i bought a king-size bed and threw the sofa one out, as we all lived on and in it anyway.

we never heard from abigail, and until i saw that picture in the gallery window thought she was gone forever. i read in the arts section of the sunday times one day she would be at the first night opening at the gallery. her lover died and left all his unsold works to her. it was a warehouse full of invaluable artworks, including nude bronze statues.

the three of us went to see her on opening night. it was like old times. afterward, the four of us jumped in the king-size bed, which wasn't as crowded as the old sofa bed.

it was good times again

4 - tomás

i was a senior about to graduate college in a few months. during the week, when there were classes, i stayed in the city at keisha's place with her and tomás.

it was late april, i only had a morning class, so i was back at the apartment by noon. there was a knocking on the door. it was the manager of the messenger service, tomás's boss.

is keishas in? he asked. *there was a serious accident on broadway this mornong, a taxi swerved, and hit tomás. he died on the way to the hospital.*

i knew she would be devastated. i waited until she came home from work to tell her. when keisha walked in, i held her close, and whispered the news; she started to cry. her tears flowed down my cheeks, soaked my shirt, and she fell to her knees in a fetal position. i called her therapist, but there was no answer and left a message; eventually, keisha went silent and just stared at the ceiling. later, she closed her eyes and went to sleep on the floor. satisfied she was now calm, i went to bed. i had an early class the next day.

my alarm went off in the morning; as i walked to the front door to go down the hall to the bathroom, i saw keisha in the kitchen area. she was on the floor in a pool of blood, wrists slashed, and a knife next to her dripping red. i knew she was gone; i called police and gave them all the personal information i knew about her. after they took her body away, i locked the door, then took the subway back to brooklyn to my parent's home.

clown car ride/squished

i hate squeezing into the little car
with eleven other clowns
in full costume –
we are packed tighter
then the fat lady's vagina;
my nose is pushed into
willie the clown's bulbous rear
after he had franks and beans
for lunch – i have been practicing
breath control these last few shows

sexy suzy the clown bride
is behind me, sliding her arm
over my body, her left hand
down my wide clown pants
as i try to push her arm off;
problem is she slides my hand away
onto fireman fred's crotch,
who thinks it is her!

i yell at mad max the clown,
our driver, *speed it up*, but he yells
something back about fuel economy!
for pete's sake, we only go fifty feet
into the center ring

mad max has a cattle prod that he zaps
my left foot with causing my body to gyrate
while sexy suzy, still amuses herself with me,
forces my body up against willie's back –

out of costume, i now realize why he has that
silly smile when he sees me

after this show, i'm going to the ringmaster
to ask to work with the lion tamer –
i want to be the guy holding the gun with
live ammunition, and when the clown car pulls up
i'm going to shoot them all,
except for madge the midget –
when i stand, she's the right height
to give me oral sex

she can live

retirement

slept from midnight
woke up
at six this morning
the wacky-weed gummy worked
3 am wake-ups are in the past
today is wednesday
nothing to do till four pm
no, today is tuesday
tomorrow is wednesday
i lose track of days
most feel like sunday
sometimes saturday feels like sunday
and friday feels like a saturday —
without my work structure
I'm lost in life
like a trained circus animal
did the same routine for decades
now free float in life
lost in the outer space of old age —
then i'll die

my neighbor's window

the orange tabby sits still, stares out,
watches while wobbly children walk, then fall,
on soft green grass that needs to be mowed
and the flower garden sways in the light breeze
as the cat watches, watches for movement
in the lawn, unable to feel the softness of the dirt yet
aware of a small rodent with thin tail trails behind as it
scurries about only feet from frolicking kids — until the
cat hears a slight sound inside, its ears perk up, causing
its head to turn, eyes to focus, and spring-like legs
uncoil with a leap down and four paws with razor-sharp
claws punctures the furry skin of a house mouse, then
plays with its prey tossing it about, the mouse knows, it
knows its fate; its time almost up unless the mistress of
the house comes in and rescues it before brown body
parts scatter on the floor after partially digested; then
the cat hops on the sofa and, with a full tummy,
falls asleep on the narrow wooden sill

a pizza place

located on a corner store in bensonhurst
in the middle of italian brooklyn
i stop in for a hot slice with pepperoni,
and a medium-sized, orange fountain soda

maria is the waitress and takes my order
red lipstick, on thick lips, attracts attention
a pushup bra with a low-cut blouse, and
teased, dyed, blond hair typically gets big tips

gold chains around her neck bounce
with every step she takes towards me
but i'm focused on her lips, chewing gum,
it draws my eyes to her juicy mouth; it's inviting

tight-stretch pants cling to curves and crevices
can't beat a server with pizazz in a pizza place
what more can a teenage boy ask for
other than she gives me her phone number

unfortunately, i don't wear enough gold, or able
to *saturday night fever* walk on 86th street —
i'm no flashy movie john travolta dancing away
but an insecure teenager, one spring afternoon

just wanting a hot slice with a cold drink

fries

the knife and fork are untouched
wrapped in a napkin on my left
i order finger food —
same order, always,
never a change
seems my hamburger is married

wherever i order it
oil-soaked, salted, long yellow potatoes
thinly sliced and fried till crisp and crunchy
tag along

they overflow the small plate
while a few hide under soft buns
ketchup spills out of the bottle
splatters on the plate
a few drops land on my shirt
and a blob sits there
like a giant red pool
right next to the fries
as it waits for first dips
then seconds

by the bottom of the fried pile
a red smear
covers most of my plate —
when there's none left
i let the dog lick it clea

lord byron, scallywag

her girlfriend jane introduces me
lois is supposed to be a moderator
for a writer's workshop group
at her home
she asks me to join
i'm not sure if it'll be a good fit
she's pleasant enough
grey hair, a few extra pounds,
maybe more than a few,
round-faced
round ass
two tires stretch out
a skintight black blouse

her friend said she's a widow
likes to read byron and keats
i tell them i like them too,
though i don't,
modern poetry is my thing,
ginsberg, o'hara, bukowski

when jane
goes upstairs for a few minutes
lois asks if i like french, as in kisses,
it's been a while since i did, i
don't wait, step forward,
her bared breast is round and full,
inviting
maybe, i misjudged the group

schmidt – the gym teacher

i never knew the gym teacher's first name
worked with him for twenty years
said hello only; i taught high school english
located in the basement was the school nurse

she ministered
to those who needed her care
there were always injured kids in the gym
scrapes, sprains, sores in need of care

schmidt, the gym teacher,
by law, has to assist a student
to the nurse's office —
he was always there

during lunchtime
the married nurse,
when her door is locked,
biblically nursed schmidt, too

lunch in manhattan

when a caffeine fix is needed
or a burger to fill an empty space
look for small shops on long blocks
with few tables and short rows of stools

coffee shops in manhattan
are ubiquitous
like feathers on birds
invisible until they flap wings

i sit at the counter with drink and muffin
a homeless man walks in, begs for a buck,
dressed in rags and an umbrella of scent
are you hungry, i'll buy you food

waitress, please seat him, I'll pay for it —
seated at a rear table away from the door
he orders something to eat and a coffee
i slip the waitress a tip, cash for the bill,

then place ten dollars on the rear table
once he starts to eat, and then i leave

west virginia coalminer

he can't cough
or breathe deeply
pink lungs at birth
soft and supple
he heated homes
kept cities' electric turbines turning
now, black lung disease
hardens tissue
rock hard
black coal and rock dust kill
at thirty-five
a retired coal miner
can't work, walk far, or
blow up his child's balloon
while to everyone else
everywhere
he is invisible
reduced to a statistic
on a page
on a government report
while the mines continue as usual

east village muse

she isn't a tall, thin model
or someone with striking looks
average   best describes her

a friend to starving artists
and unemployed, underpaid writers
she is their confidante
personally entangled with them
at all hours of the week

her simple insight
into their creativity
results in poems, stories, and
paintings of her
peddled in galleries
all over the city
for *their* fame and fortune
when not draped in a cloth
she poses unclothed
in studios or bedrooms

the unknown, become famous
some wealthy, beyond belief
while she glides through life
a hanger-on, dependent on others
lives where she can
on sofas
or next to a warm body in their bed

rue des fleurs in winter

the bluest blue-sky
shines through floor-to-ceiling glass
speckled with the tiniest flecks
of white, windblown winter snow

artic winds sweep streets clean
everything outside freezes
yet in her paris bedroom
the temperature rises fast

the easel in the corner is full
a canvas awaits her lover
the portrait. almost finished
a few more brush strokes needed

lilac-scented bed sheets rumpled
pillows moved and rearranged
the holy grail of love proceeds
her artist said she needs inspiration

a swish of movement incites as
a painter's hand carefully caresses curves
hopefully, muscle memory will paint
what two skins touch can inspire

inner turmoil

it's hard to kill your babies
hours and hours of creativity
   wasted
   erased
   gone
words fly out quickly
stanza after stanza
page after page
yet
not to my satisfaction

the delete key is red
with the blood and sweat
i spent
on this still-born piece
   never
to see it on paper

retirement

the racetrack is far in the past
now free to roam on fenced pasture
its gait slows with age
a long mane and tail turned grey
the youthful pony who races everywhere
now ambles to the barn
its riders are now walkers who lead it around
to give a tired, gentle ride
to young children on sundays

slow walks keep muscles somewhat toned
similar to the elderly woman who sits on a rocker
her working days over
the bordello in her past
she enjoyed the high life in youth
traveled far and wide as a paid companion
gifts of jewelry and cash, five-star dinners
her body the eye candy wealthy men cherished
now relegated to high tea instead of cocktails
she lives at her madam's house, who is her lover,
works a little if a granny requested
life is not always easy
when the finality of life approaches

john and yoko

time clears the fog
of the presence
we lived through

it allows us to clearly see
what we misunderstood
while enduring our past

and finally understand
the creativity and brilliance
hidden by a slanted media

from years ago; and
to truly appreciate
their lives, love, and

performance art
they tried to infuse
into our ordinary life

republican abortion bans

laws kill
the never convicted

never tried
yet she died

on a kitchen table
poor

pregnant no more
left behind four kids

politicians don't care
they can pay airfare

karma kills

michael stands and watches
as the plane glides down the runway
faster
  faster   *finally* *airborne*

he cranks his head skyward
watches air melt and distort behind
as blue clouds seem to float softly
going nowhere stationary in the air
as a flock of canada geese flew at the plane
the jet sucks them into the single-engine
flames appear, smoke billows out the exhaust
the plane sputters
   then

     falls to the ground
  explodes in a fireball
he smiles ear to ear
his business partner
was on the plane to las vegas
to marry michael's ex-wife
with whom he had a year's-long affair
 after the divorce was finalized yesterday

a large life insurance policy
was recently purchased
on all the business partners
for legitimate reasons

sometimes life hurts
sometimes it doesn't

summer storm

we were young
only teenagers
school restarts soon
it was a summer romance
we met at a lake resort
its memories live forever —
as the rain started
a torrential downpour
while we embraced,
a kiss with unwedded bliss
i still remember
under tall forest trees
drops heavy, pitter-patter on leaves
our blanket soaked
as wet bodies
squeezed out water
from between us
while wind tried to chill
but body heat kept us warm
our love would last an eternity
we thought

but it was only a summer romance
those many years ago

freedom

i took the ferry
from battery park
to liberty island
the statue is there
a gift from france
it doesn't speak french tho
green
tall
big feet
big torch
stands in the harbor
greets all
looks down at tiny people
silently

yet they know
    they know
just to see her
up close   or afar
    they know

summer day in july

sigh
on the boardwalk this morning
hot and humid
sand everywhere
young women in barely bikinis
play volleyball, bounce around
on the soft sand ground

sigh
old men still have eyesight
still mentally a teen
feel hopeless and helpless

sigh
why look at them
        useless
bad knees, barely walk two blocks
sparks in the mind's engine, ready to ignite
but the tinder won't light
machinery's tired
used excessively for years
now retired

sigh
rumble in the bumble fruitless
ignition is shot
past its useful life
leave it be by itself
resting quietly
till put away and forgotten, forever
maybe some parts recycled

sigh

rumor of christine and philip 1961

boddingtons pale ale, please
a princely request said with a tease
she smiled her gracious smile
with the knowledge of later coming

secreted behind a closed door
only a rumor lives on of the whore
and the royal she might fully screw
yet he was not first in her queue

ministers and spies were there first
her appetite had a very big thirst
and a picture on the news's front page
made this young girl the ultimate rage

no one knows if the rumor is true
the scandal was quite sexy, and blue
these men are now buried and dead
their secrets forever hidden within her bed

a one-eared pirate

wait for a hot summer sun
to put the virus on the run
virus killed a million dead
not one tear did he shed

no one was truly safe
many of his aids
walked the plank for him
he led a life of dreadful sin

walk with me to the capital
intent to rule forever
hang his next in command
who refused to do his bidding

led a ragtag army
in a rebellion that day
against law and order
so he can continue to plunder

defeated, he lied and lied
caught, his freedom now tied
in court after court, he fought
to wiggle out of jail, he tried

big news in a tiny rural town

    one inch
not a lot of area
most thumbs are larger
    one inch
a tiny measure with a big impact
life or death importance
    one inch
is the difference
a past president lives
    one inch
grazed an ear
by such a small space
    one inch
could have changed
an election

after vacation

writing stops
creativity flatlines
editors try to doctor a piece
    nothing helps
the poet would even settle
for an injection of rhyme
but the cemetery of words
overflows with buried stanzas

it waits for resurrection
to come alive again
bloom with freshness
stirs latent muses
who succumbed
to other interests
in a fast-moving world
of ideas

july thunderstorm

the potted flowers on my front lawn
sway in a storm's powerful gusts
water overflows from the rims
stems bent, too weak to stand tall

later, when the sunshine arrives
the heat dries the street, humidity rises
along with the pretty flowers now unbent
at least those with petals left to please

i have friends
who weathered their storms
powerful drugs tried to unbend broken bodies
to allow them to stand tall again in life

a few i knew
could not wait for their sunshine
they fell, bent, and damaged
beyond repair, beyond despair
forever gone, like blown-away petals

awkward romance

in a manhattan loft
on tenth-avenue midtown
they're in bed together —
finished
she sits up
reaches for a joint
    lights up
    inhales twice
    shares it
    since he bought the weed
i love you   she whispers
it is a third date
he thinks
    this is only dinner payback, fun, not love
then he reaches for a roach clip
to finish it off
not hearing those words returned
    silence
    she waits
    and waits
        then asks if he loves her

a minute drags by
then gives his excuse
i am married
and can't commit to you fully

i don't care
i am too

green grass gone 1960's

in the backwoods
near stanhope, new jersey
by the old, over-worked,
abandoned iron mines
is a lover's lane
hidden from the world
in a dense, scrub pine forest
until you get to the small pasture
where the ground is littered
with drained beer and wine bottles
and the darling's used detritus
strewn like snowflakes
on the ground,
on tree branches,
near the filled-in old morris canal
where boats brought iron ore
to the hudson river ports
in jersey city —
now, it sustains personal procreation
instead of commercial flotation

wasted death

there are so many of them
young men and women
who never achieve in a career
or nurse a newborn in their arms
dead before their allotted time
killed by old men for political reasons
sent to war to kill and maim
until they succumb
on distant death-soiled dirt

mixologist

shaved head, large hoop earrings
sharp and smart as a whip
with a sense of unparalleled humor
larger than her five-foot frame

they had a meeting of the minds
saw humor in the same things
many laughs shared led to a friendship,
eventually, discrete meetings

her light mocha skin blends in
when his white arm wraps around
her and rests by her neck   atop a pillow
in her small studio apartment

divorced, it was bitter, heartbreaking,
she was only married for one year
when her husband decided he wanted others —
alone, she had to rebuild her life back

they stumbled into one another at a party
they knew it was only a love fling
he could not commit as he was, already,
but he offered emotional support   and

she adored him as a strong, stiff oak tree
there for her to lean on when needed   and
to offer protective shade when her dating life
became hot, nerves too intense to continue

submission purgatory

wait for it
wait a little longer
the submission response will come
someday
      soon
               maybe
creativity flourished
gurgled out onto blank spaces
with innate brilliance
hopeful it hits home
with an unknown editor
who sits
in a windowless, unknown office
stares at a computer screen
all-day
every day
until days end
eyes bleary, strained, tired
maybe the accept key
will spit out a letter
eight months after the initial receipt
maybe

goodbye weird donny

dead, finality,
stuffed like a burger sandwich
with pickles, onions, ketchup
on a sesame seed roll
into a big, beautiful big box
a bigger box than anyone
the biggest ever made
now buried after a preacher
says one nice thing, not more,
they rush to slam the coffin's door

everyone tattled when he was alive
about his many legal woes that dived
they're not buried, too
but openly spoken about:
    his lovers on the side,
    taxes never paid,
    crimes convicted, finally found

the holy man spits out platitudes
not aware of the many prostitutes
or the deceased negative attitudes
when a mean man finally dies
not one normal person cries —
his whole life, he only told lies

stalled in newark

a young black girl
in an urban burned-out city
with a future
as dark as her skin

under-sourced schools
guarantee failure
hungry, semi-literate,
students potential bridled

branded as failures
due to location, crime
and political incompetence;
not   ability

because
people with educational blinders
cannot successfully race in life
and a girl's future shackled

to the baptist church cemetery
her potter's plot reserved at birth
waits for her to enter
not in old age   but any day

if god were a woman

there would be no war
she could not bear
her children
maimed, killed, tortured
or the poor
denied medical help
or food
in her name

a mother cares

therefore
god is not a woman
but a tool for cruelty
by cold-hearted men
with a passion for destruction
and self-preservation
with no pity or compassion
for those less fortunate

fun on a summer day

i have to find the right one
not too big
not too round
not too bumpy
one side has to be kinda flat and smooth
it's not easy anymore
my eyesight isn't what it once was
then i found it
close to the shore
half buried in mud
washed it off
gripped it in my fingers
then, with a side-arm throw
the perfect stone
slid perfectly
across a pristine pond of still water
all the way across
skips up and down on the liquid top
twenty, thirty, almost forty feet
stops; sinks to the bottom
        for eternity

then i look for another stone

is it possible

can words be beautiful
would stanzas of rhyme
sweeten my days' time

are sugary lines
more tasteful
than visual

poetry melds reality
into a world of taste
hopefully   well done

mississippi back-alley doctor

he was their last resort
cheap fees   cash only
doesn't accept insurance
only available through referrals

his office, a cheap motel room
hidden
on the other side of the tracks, and a
medical degree from an online video

sterile tools from a knitting store
and illegal certification to operate
from law firm of clarence, samuel, and brett
and old weirdo-donald   who really doesn't care

some patients bled to death
a few died from sepsis
handfuls lived sterile lives after, and
none forgot the trauma of that day

the religious right politicians fought to save
an unborn life that is not yet alive
conveniently forgot past years of suffering
and avoidable deaths of expectant women

dick and jane after trumps debate

run dick run
run jane run
jane, grab the cats
you grab the dogs, dick
immigrants are coming
jane, grab the goats
you grab the parrots, dick
immigrants are coming
old don-**old** said they're eating pets
he said he saw it on television
hurry, save them all
immigrants are coming

back seat 1959

over sixty years ago
in my mom's compact car
one moonlit night
parked in a clearing
on top of the forested hill
by our summer home
in rural northwest new jersey
on lake hopatcong
both fifteen
i don't remember the car
color
make
or its year
but the cramped space
for two teenagers
to be intimate
i vividly remember

also, the girl —
one of the first in life
is always remembered

my world is in tears

i couldn't believe it
the stairwell between floors
buzz
as students rush up and down steps
to get to the next class
when someone shouts out
president kennedy was shot in dallas

my world momentarily halts
all the students seem to freeze
their eyes well up
girls' tear-stained makeup smears
every thing is in slow motion

the rest of that day
is blurry
camelot is lanced through the heart
blood-soaked jackie looks on
as lyndon johnson sworn in

the sweet lyrics to life's song
turns sour with sorrow
how can my worldly security be restored —
more than a president died
that fateful day in texas

a nation's innocence
was pierced

her pictures on social media

tell me everything —
after years of wondering
i now know
she's moved on

my useless lamentations
our romance years ago
will always be a memory
of what could have been

if only she were content
with normalcy
but a wild child
never settles down

the universe shined
its spotlight on her
as she dances to a tune
most don't hear

but we can watch
amazed with open jaws
envious of her abandonment
of life's societal restrictions

lives free and unburdened
into adulthood and old age

extinct

as i grew older
my innocence died
it no longer exists
the kindness and simple love of youth
replaced by:
   politicians' wars
   terrorist killings
   betrayals by trusted friends
   many psychopaths' threats
   mob-connected brooklyn customers
   corrupt city police
   cash grabbing inspectors
have hardened me
my youthful, simplistic innocence
buried
with maturity

king of the roaches

he thrives on slime, uncouthness
ignores harmful disease, and
brings sickness to society

grows rich in muck
to lead the colony
through filth and garbage

as leader of the roaches
he has a mate who is
his third consecutive one

while behind a warm oven
in a golf course country club kitchen
he dalliances

with a femme fatale
he tells his swarm of followers
stand back and stand by

then pays his new conquest
thousands of rotted banana peels
to sign a nondisclosure agreement

only in america

respect

the two-by-four
is placed on opposite sawhorses
   s l o w l y
bricks are placed in the center
one upon the one below
until it sags
then splits
like the husband who walks out
to leave a wife behind
after decades together —
she never appreciated his work
either ignored
or denigrated it
until the last brick
broke
    the
      marriage

one

one dollar
equals
one hundred pennies
multiply it by adding zeros
it can buy
literally
everything material
but it can't purchase kindness
without someone with empathy
spending it with care in mind
yet certain politicians
in their infinite wisdom
refuse to spend it to help
  sickly people
  children in need of food
  educate everyone to their best abilities
pennies add up
that's why they cut taxes for the wealthy
knowing the undereducated
don't know any better
and vote for long-term tax cuts
harming themselves
when their one vote
can change everything

sinthia the poet

soft-spoken and single
lives home with family
a reserved,
demure,
proper person,
until her written words
   explode
with the flames in her hearth and
coals of lust stroke hot
as her loins throb on paper
with female pheromones
   yearning
for an intended lover's tender touch
while she beckons him
to recline with her
on crimson, smooth silk sheets,
to be ravished
until, with her last breath,
she moans with ecstasy
   exhausted

death of a loved one

death has a permanence to it
you don't see the person anymore
nor
   speak to them
   hear them
   touch them
death is the finality of life

my daughter is separated
her fourteen-year-old son
decided to stay with his father
who always plays sports with him

i don't
   see him anymore
   hear his voice
   touch his arm
   hug his body
   kiss his cheek
   receive his texts
sadly
    i feel dead

loose change

my pockets jingle jangle
with a handful of coins
somehow reminds me
of my family today

years ago, we were a solid dollar
together in our home
breakfast and dinner as a group
weekend sports in tandem

today, they are out and about
my home is empty
silence bounces off the walls
echoes of sounds remain in-mind

the children scattered all over
north, south, east, everywhere
except in their old homestead
like the change in all my pockets

friendship

after i speak to a long-distance friend
grey skies linger over her house
she suffers from an unknown illness
and hopefully, tomorrow will be better

window shades pulled down
as a storm percolates on her life
the heavens rumble with thunder
my sadness intensifies for my friend

her mental anguish disturbs me
nice people should not needlessly suffer
there are enough nasty folks to choose from
why should a marital abuse survivor be the one

my sad heart is filled with dark clouds
blacker than the gloomy sky outside

it is incurable

his time is limited
their love strong and long
too quickly, years flew past
now slow walks
with short talks
meaningful words
they speak about death
he doesn't believe in heaven
after his last breath
ashes in a bag
bone and dust
she pours it in a vase
some sticks on fingers
it tastes salty
like the ocean he adored
slowly
forever
he becomes a part of her

change

i got me a new gal
since the old one left
with both arms
she clutched clothes
then bussed back north
to a bustling big city
my downhome style
wasn't her thing
only wore high heels
everywhere we went

my new squeeze is country
from y'all to chuggin' bar beer
she plows my fields
on a john deere
and shovels stalls
down to the wood
i popped the question
she said she would

getting along

new york is a large city
different strata of people
try to co-exist lawfully
except for the underbelly
of society who inhabit the
sewers of humanity

the dark streets and avenues
where not many live or work
when the sun goes down
burst alive with cars on a slow troll
where nearly nude women stroll
while pimps propped in shadowy doorways
as their holes work the black asphalt

police cars glide past but don't stop
except on the corners for their cash tips
to keep things quiet on the streets
yet inside cars and trucks, wildness rules
sex for sale at discount rate specials
pay the girls, and you live to tell of it

pretty people party

at a penthouse
in midtown manhattan
a party's happening
with beautiful people
torn from fashion magazines
strutting in high-end clothes
while servers serve hot hors d'oeuvres
to guests who indulge
in small talk gossip
about ephemeral issues
when minutes before sunset
a woman's voice is heard
loudly moaning
it draws a crowd
to the northern railing
they look down one flight
to an offset balcony
where a naked couple
are entangled on a chaise
in flagrante delicto
oblivious
to an attractive audience above
who became peeping toms
as a semi-famous model
left the sunroof, followed
by an aging broadway actor
to disappear into an available bedroom
in the rear of the apartment
on top of full-length mink coats

abortion

swat them
quickly
those blood-suckers

female mosquitos
drink human blood
to feed their eggs

we are all abortionists
we are all colors and creeds
from very religious to non-believers

our hemoglobin
has the proteins
needed for growth

every time you swat one
feasting on your body
you are killing their unborn

if life is sacred
a gift from god,
is a small life

different
than a big life?
is the question

born free

a short drive from boulder, colorado
parallel to the front range
i look out my car window eastward
to america's great plains
they stretch green
as far as the eye can see
until absorbed by the horizon

big sky country is amazing,
it never ends; i arrive
in wyoming
where wild mustangs
still roam free

they're beautiful beasts
all colors, unhampered,
i notice a couple
parked ahead
on the side of the road
with a horse trailer attached

they had bought
a tamed wild mustang
years ago at auction
and are going to ride it
once more, as it's much older now,
on the grasslands where it was born —
guess you can go home again

smell rain

stay inside
as she sniffs the air
it's going to rain

although the sun shines bright
through shadeless windows
in early morning
she romantically entices him
to remain in bed

suddenly, the roof shook violently
thunder roared above
heaven's faucet opens
torrential downpours deluge everything
a flash flood flushes down hills

muddy water becomes rampaging rapids
as cars swept away
while homes, damaged, collapse —
people who venture out
are hurt as debris flows past
while inside their brick house
they embrace in marital junction

married lovers

after sundown
quickie motels pop alive
on dark side streets
in desolate areas of town
as cars park and leave
and rooms turn over
every three hours

where married lovers
are supposed to be working late
throw off a befouled bed's blankets
then tuesday's work clothes
to playdate a marriage
for a few
sexually sinful moments
of prohibited
at-home intimate activities

they dress, then return
to respective spouses
and finish their workday
home to a loving family

struggles

many people believe
a deity is
  all-powerful
   yet unknown
     beyond comprehension
      to be known
because faith is a belief
based on indoctrination
while reality, in life, is chaos
as we try to give it order
and struggle
to fall in line
and blend with everyone else
to not be ostracized
as a free thinker or radical
because every church
wants worker ants
to follow
   unquestioning
their sweet tales and blind trails
of unneeded redemption

supermarket schpillkiss

damn old people
what a pain in the ass some are
supermarket lines are long
he places four frozen ice cream boxes,
six large two-liter sodas,
and slowly counts out
pennies, nickels, and dimes
on the conveyor —
the belt moves forward
he pays with a credit card
the old, grey-haired lady cashier
s l o w l y picks up his coins
as he asks for a one-dollar bill back

sorry, but you charged your order
the register won't open now

s l o w l y she counts the change
then gives it back to him
his wife appears
chastises him

we're going out to eat tonight
why would you give away coins
standing there, they discuss it
while i wait in line
in front of five others

pride month

thinks he is saving her
from what, she never thought
the bible thumper's a burr
his efforts are for naught

her clothes are what *she* likes
flashy, loud, and very bright
they attract a lot of dikes
she is   a breathtaking sight

conservatives want their values
observed by the rest of the world
her lifestyle, they openly refuse
            then defuse
when their daughter marries a girl

destination since childhood

her trip was not planned
though eventually expected
as all adults eventually do

it appears over the horizon
to beckon with silence
a promise of peace and serenity

where she can walk freely
run with the wind
swim over world seas

and watch from above
as loved ones below
mourn her death

street art

some draw on the sidewalks
others on black asphalt
but the real action is fleeting
like washed-away chalk
it's real-life people
who do crazy stunts
then disperse into a crowd
they leave no trace
but a memory
of broken romances
leave heartache,
unfulfilled dreams and desires
to ruminate on for years

true love

does not need eyes
it doesn't see
    skin color
    weight
    height
only a person's soul
needs to shine

except sometimes
its brightness and beauty
attracts lovers
like bears to honey
to engulf in throes
of an agonizing death
some call a fatal attraction
to be strung out for eternity
as in some marriages

bridal march

the ceremony will begin soon
nerves are tingling
groomsmen smile and cheer
straighten bowties and drink a beer

bridesmaids' hair sprayed and sheared
makeup applied, will not be smeared
parents are happy and smiles galore
except the bride feels like a whore

an arranged marriage is about to take place
the bride is forced to put a smile on her face
her dowery was paid in cash and gold bars
the ceremony will start once they see three stars

she's cold, shivers, puts on an old sweater,
was praying for snow and very bad weather
anything to prevent this forced upon marriage
it's not love but a love-life miscarriage

music starts, and the wedding party goes forth
left in the lobby, last to walk down
she turns to the doors, heads out to far north
doesn't want to marry a much older clown

she's seventeen, in love with being in love
he's thirty-five and just bought a young wife
like a freed bird, she flew like a dove
left him upset, with almost married strife

closeted hollywood

he was like a beautiful gift
in a wrapped box
with multicolored paper and
a large pink bow on top

when it was time
to open the carton
shards of gift wrap scatter about
as flaps finally flip

he comes out to the world
people yawn
it's old news
to those who assumed

too nice

a sweet old lady
full of sugary syrup
probably maple

she's in vermont, frail,
stooped, short white hair
undone and wild

her family gone
only pictures in albums
keep them alive   for herself

gone
they constantly haunt her
all hours of awakeness

dementia held at bay
in the future, someday,
but not today

ozempic thin

he didn't know her from before
when she had an oval shape
almost round,
with thick arms and thighs
two small, perfectly shaped a-cup breasts
her female treasure buried
deep within fat folds
hidden from view
now exposed
for lovers to plunder
and ignore the saggy pancakes on her chest
while flaps of skin hang from both lower hips

next week is the operation
to remove it, tuck it, tighten
a body rarely seen by the sun
now exposed on naturist beaches
absorbing hot rays of summer and
cool splashes of salty waves
to attract a never-ending line
of potential lovers
her mattress needs to be changed
no bounce left
because now, she is in her prime
and life is good

the bottle

it's an amber-colored glass
desired by many
who need to hit the bottle
not to break it
but to drink it
its contents a smoother of grief
and the cause of anguish
a cursed addiction when wet
hard to dry out forever
its contents bring sleep
sometimes anger
sometimes forgetfulness
better to hide the bottle
than empty it

less problems

if you see my mother, say hello

i wanted to say this to him
before he died
    but i didn't
i knew him slightly from the block
a nasty bully who picked on kids,
hit them and stole their lunch money —
there was nothing to like about him
    nothing at all
and when the large dump trunk hit him,
splattered his body under 18 huge black wheels
in front of cathy's corner candy store, and
the daily newspaper display atop a steel rack on the
sidewalk was blood-stained
with tiny red droplets on the front page
on black ink —
i wanted to tell his remains
to say hello to my mother
but i didn't
because i knew
        he wasn't going
            to heaven

cold day to grieve

it is the dead of winter
no summer songs or fancy flowers
no whirling westerly winds blowing
or young lovers loving outdoors

rock-hard frozen ground
fights the digger's steel shovels,
husbanding dirt while a casket
needs to wait

men struggle to break topsoil
pile it on a new found mound
with the grieving family
in black, tears stream, they wait

a solitary black crow craws loudly
from atop a nearby tombstone
and watches peaceful earth
accept its intrusion, and refilled dirt

bump

most people think a bump
is a problem
sometimes, they get over it
or around it

but a baby bump
can be a joyful thing
usually not a problem
  unless unplanned

what is a young girl to do
moments have consequences
now, a lifetime of seconds ahead,
trying and crying all too often

focus and dedication might work
easy-street now but a dream
years ahead of intensity test her mettle
she'll get ahead if she doesn't settle

halloween fright night

midnight approaches
moonlight barely shines
cemetery gates creak open
burial plots percolate
as the doomed
wake from slumber

slowly they walk
to the entrance
seek revenge
on the faithful
who condemned them
to eternity
in the ovens of below earth
where angels never venture
and lilith rules beyond reproach

tonight, her minions venture forth
intent on a death march
while outside the gate
zombie killers wait in ambush
loaded with ectoplasmic weapons
in a last-ditch attempt
to save humanity

only sunrise can stop the slaughter

he waited

at forty-two
married
he had a year's patience
with an employee
until she turned eighteen

the girl was a flirt
teased the boys
then followed through
experienced in affection
her fun reputation was perfection

after her birthday
he succumbed
every tuesday afternoon
for months and months
every desire satisfied
every raise request gratified
until she broke it off
and quit her job

a year later at nineteen
she married
a forty-five-year-old man
and never had to work again

follicles

at sixteen
my follicles said goodbye
long curls
a ponytail
my brush collected hair
like an avid stamp collector

now baldness is becoming

sometimes
hats became required
in winter, summer,
spring and fall
until i met a young girl
bald from chemo

my chapeaus now sit
on a shelf
in solidarity

pass the torch

she was single, irish, forty-five
tall and thin, brunette with long hair
a certain easiness about her as
she spoke with a delightful, lilting brogue

one night at a party, he walked in,
their eyes met, in air love crossed
twenty-eight, hair curly-tossed
rugged, a sculptor, he was her desires

a twenty-year difference never existed
they traveled together for years
everywhere, never apart, truly in love
she never thought they would ever part

but at one point he wanted children
now, she's almost sixty, it wasn't possible;
one day, she met a young, curly-haired
blond woman, they became fast friends

she introduced her to him one night
at a friend's wine party in dublin
she saw sparks in their eyes
quietly, she walked out, didn't say goodbye

years later, she notices his work is showing
in a local gallery, and is going to see him
when she walks in, a small, blond, curly-haired girl runs
up to her *mommy said you're her friend*

daddy said he loved you and mommy a lot
before he died last year

a kyrielle[1]

it happened in a summer camp
month end we had a party romp
everyone had to costume up
to see the girls change in their clothes

naked girls, young boys want to see
long as they don't chance to see me
through the wall hole, i must see three
to see the girls change in their clothes

thirteen, I knew it wasn't right
but hormones have a very strange might
forcing boys to lust for the sight
to see the girls change in their clothes

---

[1] A french form of poetry

olympic's one-tenth second

so small
yet a canyon in life

winners win
by a splith of a second

losers lose
by a splith of a point

and not be pictured
on a cereal box

one-tenth second
is worth millions

waves

life is like the seven seas
it comes in waves
some smoother
others, big and bold,
hurricane strength
which tests our mettle

do we collapse and drown
let life sink us
                    to the
                            bottom
or float on top 'til land

we'll never know
what the next tide brings\
this is the mystery of life
and its beauty

guiding hand

3 am writing on hot, humid summer nights, groggy with
sleep, eyes strain open to peep, the blank page beckons,
it waits for inspiration when i feel a presence; a poet's
ghost visits me, the window faces my neighbor —
also up and walking around naked — when i feel
bukowski's presence take my hand, he whispers in my
ear: *write about her, all about her, why her husband left,*
her saggy breasts, the men who visit throughout the
night and park their cars blocking driveways and leave
empty beer bottles on the grass, and the time she asked
you to help her in the house for a little while, but you
chickened out —
suddenly, thoughts pour on the page, stanza after
stanza, lines begin to appear, i write words and
descriptions i would never do without his guidance and
encouragement
then silence,

he left
quietly and quickly

my writing stops

she told me

it isn't easy being easy
too many boys tried to be men
left her wondering
left her wanting
misguided in life

a search for love
took her to wrong places
where will she find   *the one*
who can be gentle, satisfying
yet have a heart of empathy
to care for her, all of her,
because
life is too short to be left adrift
without a safe port to drop anchor

camping in a sleeping bag

to hike up steep slopes
is my desire
the bigger, the better
until i tire after a trudge

underbrush is dense
i persevere
through the thickets
overhanging heights ahead

pinnacle within sight
i urge my body onward
goal almost achieved
the mountains majestic

this is my first date with her

routine

this morning
is like the others
an early walk alone
in the woods
i smell sweet dew burn off
as the sun strengthens
and birds flutter
in the leaves above —
usually
nobody is here with me —
in afternoons
the trail can be busier
but right now,
trees keep me company
until i come
to an off-trail path
leading to a meadow
hidden from view
where i spend
a few moments in silence
as i walk in the tall grass —
on the open space
that once heard giggles
of a young kid playing ball
with our family dog

last year i spread
my child's ashes here

moving day

the walls are bare
pictures boxed
ready to go
furniture gone
carpet indents historical reminders
rooms echo silence
except where floorboards squeak
when i walk slowly on them
to inspect everything
before i lock the door
permanently
for one last time

only the ghosts of family remain

aging

as i get older
packages seem heavier

the walk to the mailbox
used to be a
hop,
skip, and
jump

now, it's a slow walk
with a
      stop
           on the way

as for running
well, let's not go there

getting mail
is not an athletic endeavor

postal service

snail mail is terribly slow
used to be a day or two
now i wait by the curb
muttering to myself *nuu, nuu*

in reality, that's really quick
my son took a full nine months
till i received his expected delivery
and held him tenderly in my arms

letters are a few ounces
he was five pounds eleven
in my hands, a piece of heaven
i had to wait for him to leaven

valery messalina [2]

has a runaway libido
she's the elderly man's third wife,
when her husband passes out
from his many nightly scotches
she sneaks out to work out
at the downstairs gym
to engage and engorge younger men —
this went on for months
until her lovers begin to appear
everywhere
there are so many;
during boring days
she works as a high-end escort

one evening when he
is away in california on business
she went out at night
to enjoy her secret work schedule
for extra cash and conjugal fun;
with another co-working girl
they have a date for two
in a midtown manhattan hotel
as she enters the bridal suite
her husband stands there naked

---

[2] Valeria Messalina was the third wife of Roman
emperor Claudius. A powerful and influential woman with a
reputation for promiscuity, and was eventually executed.

the debate

run dick run
run jane run
grab the cats, jane
grab the dogs, dick

illegal immigrants are coming

grab the goats, jane
grab the parrots, dick

illegal immigrants are coming

crazy donOld said they're eating pets
he said he saw it on television
hurry, save everyone's pets

illegal immigrants are coming

visiting grandma

on the plane to iowa
a little girl sits alone
next to a big, burly man
in the aisle seat

she sings softly to herself
a song for her grandma
who always loves to hear her
the song asks

where are you going, granny
i'm coming to sing for you
the man heard the song
and inquisitively asks

if her parents
are going to visit, too
no, they are already there
they're making arrangements

114

third place

everyone wants to be in a first place
it usually is their home
a second place could be at work
and third place is the other place you go

a neighborhood bar to meet friends
or cafe for quick breakfast and coffee
or a wood bench in a park under shady leaves
where you meet someone special in shadows

then a hotel room welcomes lovers
where forbidden fruit is consumed
picked off of a forest's tree of lust
by a hungry adam and eve

third place, in reality, is not the last
but first in fond memories of the past

unnamed girl

divorced, it wasn't a pleasant experience
she was only married one year
when her husband decided he wanted others —
alone, she built her life back

shaved head, large hoop earrings
smart as a whip
with an unparalleled sense of humor
larger than her short, five-foot frame

she met this fair-haired adonis
they saw humor in similar things
many laughs shared led to friendship,
eventually, discrete meetings

her light brown skin blends in
when a muscular white arm wraps around
her beautiful head
then rests by her neck   atop a pillow

they stumbled into one another
knowing it was only a love fling   because
he could not commit as he was already,
but he offered emotional support   and

she adored him as a strong oak tree
for her to lean on when she needs help
and to offer protective shade when her life
occasionally became too hot and intense

how do you forgive

the unforgivable
or un-remember
terrible memories

tragedy happens
sometimes explainable
usually not logically

an overripe banana
can't be ripe again
brown decay's too far gone

a burial plot in a mind's cemetery
accepts the pain
to bury it

to then return to life

submission purgatory

poets write poetry
creatively splice words
into lines and stanzas
their past existence
into a poem
souls totally bare
to submit it somewhere

the pinnacle mags
only publish a few
they selectively sort
not in haste or deadline due
why rush
they have so many

a decision takes time
sometimes too long
poets can tire
a few even expire
before
a rejection letter arrives

neighbors

long ago
when i was young and just married
next door to me
lived a young couple
he worked in manhattan
manly muscles steroid strong
everywhere on his body
but at work, his fingers only held scissors

she was tall, blond, light pale skin
an inner-city high school teacher
who tutors students
in need, in her home, in her bed
for a special seventeen-year-old boy

a large custom painting
of the couple hangs on their wall
she paid for it years ago; was done
where his face could be painted over,
she said, in jest one day to me
in case she gets a new husband

their divorce was not a surprise

dead end job

it's a job
pays well
no way to advance
in a decayed city
tedious manual work

the mattress factory hums
sewers sew
he attaches the seams
Juanita sews fabric
around cording
for him to attach the top to the sides

they met at lunch a few months back
now they date
she keeps an eye on him
knows he eyes other sewers
if he makes a move on a girl
trouble will boil over
a gun's in her pocketbook

five o'clock bell rings
factory turns off
silence
they leave together
love is tough
tough love is even worse
when a jealous lover meets a competitor
on the sidewalk outside the plant

drifter

short, blond, busty
her red Cadillac is home
she travels the east coast

a few nights dancing
here, there, everywhere
entertaining men in clubs

no longer married
mom watches her kid
while she works the jerks

late nights in seedy places
big play dates in private rooms
her pay stuffed in secure spaces

her attack dog sits in the car
trained to protect near and far
it watches her stash of cash

many nights with nasty cat fights
she sleeps in a nearby no-tell motel
heads out tomorrow at noon

leaves broken hearts
quick love forever will doom
when she leaves a club's VIP room

open road leads to nowhere
her life's goals are short-sighted
next joint will also be blighted

boys

are like two-sided coins
the good side's boring, a
mild-mannered milk-toast
personality
like faded wallpaper
they're there   unnoticed

the flip side's trouble
when bad boys
drive good girls, gooney
and they do things
quietly, forbidden, hidden,
from sight
hopefully secreted forever

hope mom never finds out

until her daughter
runs with the devil
has a tummy growth fright
and her clothes are tight

then all hell breaks out

diseased

it's really big and round
seven continents of ground
the seas polluted with junk
low tides smell like skunk

used to be god's clean world
bounty's plundered, not squirreled
ozone layer flittered away
the sun heats up every day

stay inside kids, learn to play
outside causes cancer, they say
when protective layer goes away
we all will die on that day

what good are corporate profits
climate change is here to stay

dither

come hither heather
try not to dither
i see your legs aquiver
i'm sweating a river
pull down your zipper
someone needs a trimmer
as the light gets dimmer
i know what to eat for dinner
and it's not chicken

it's early evening

met her a minute ago
she boards a train
with a one-way ticket
too deep in my heart

i finally left
my old luggage
on the station platform
decided to start over

with a fresh start
i went where i
always wanted to go
with no return ticket

juicy fruit

peaches are fun to eat
take one bite
sweet juices
slide down my tongue
it's a summer sweetness
on a hot july day
while i sit
next to my sweetie
on the warm ground
under a tall shade tree
on the edge
of the farmer's field
as migrants pick peaches
place them gingerly
in a straw basket
to be packed later
then shipped all over —
i spit out the pit
and dry it off
    maybe
when i get home
i'll plant it in my backyard, and
hopefully, in a few years,
have my own small orchard
steps from my back door

i did what?

monday, early morning
the text message woke him —
good morning,
you don't know me
but i would like to speak to you
about a woman you dated
twenty years ago

he is now married with children
never cheats on his wife
works every day
can't think what this is about
he debates if he should answer —
yes, he dated a lot years ago
but that is ancient history
finally texts back, *good morning*
his phone comes alive, unknown caller

hello, how can i help you
i know this is an unusual call, but i believe
you are my father   years ago, you dated my
mother and got her pregnant
who is your mother
maria teresa silkcono
i don't remember dating anyone with that name
aren't you paulie penitto jr. from brooklyn
no, my name is pastor salvatore angelica from the
bronx
oops, so sorry, my bad

the end

Thank you for reading

More of elliot m rubin's books are
available on his website:

www.CreativeFiction.net

and follow him on Instagram at
elliot_m_rubin
people poems

www.ingramcontent.com/pod-product-compliance
Lightning Source LLC
Chambersburg PA
CBHW061655120626
46550CB00003B/951